A Child's History of Britain

Life in
Stuart Britain

Anita Ganeri

Raintree is an imprint of Capstone Global Library Limited, a company incorporated in England and Wales having its registered office at 7 Pilgrim Street, London, EC4V 6LB – Registered company number: 6695582

www.raintreepublishers.co.uk
myorders@raintreepublishers.co.uk

Edited by Nick Hunter and Penny West
Designed by Joanna Malivoire
Original illustration © Capstone Global Library Ltd 2014
Illustrated by: Laszlo Veres (pp.26-7), Beehive Illustration
Picture research by Mica Brancic
Originated by Capstone Global Library Ltd
Production by Helen McCreath
Printed and bound in China

ISBN 978 1 406 27052 5 (hardback)
18 17 16 15 14
10 9 8 7 6 5 4 3 2 1

ISBN 978 1 406 27060 0 (paperback)
19 18 17 16 15
10 9 8 7 6 5 4 3 2 1

British Library Cataloguing in Publication Data
A full catalogue record for this book is available from the British Library.

Acknowledgements
We would like to thank the following for permission to reproduce photographs: AKG-images pp. 12 (Erich Lessing), 14, 20; Alamy pp. 5 left (© Mary Evans Picture Library), 5 right (© Mary Evans Picture Library), 6 (© Oxford Events Photography), 10 (© Stuart Yates), 11 (© David Warren), 13 (© Photos 12), 15 (© Universal Images Group Limited), 22 (© Lebrecht Music and Arts Photo Library), 23 (© Mary Evans Picture Library); Corbis p. 8 (© The Print Collector); Getty Images pp. 7 (Hulton Archive), 9 (The Bridgeman Art Library/ English School), 16 (Hulton Archive), 17 (MPI), 18 (De Agostini), 21 (Hulton Archive), 24 (Archive Photos/Stock Montage), 25 (The Bridgeman Art Library/Sir James Thornhill), 27 bottom (Universal Images Group); Mary Evans Picture Library p. 19; The Picturedesk p. 27 top (The Art Archive/Museum of London).

Cover photograph of Lady Tasburgh of Bodney, Norfolk, and her children reproduced with permission of Corbis (© The Gallery Collection).

We would like to thank Heather Montgomery for her invaluable help in the preparation of this book.

Every effort has been made to contact copyright holders of material reproduced in this book. Any omissions will be rectified in subsequent printings if notice is given to the publishers.

Contents

Some words are shown in bold, **like this**. You can find out what they mean by looking in the glossary.

Stuart Britain

When Elizabeth I died in 1603, the rule of the **Tudors** came to an end. The English throne passed to Elizabeth's Scottish relative, James Stuart. He was James VI of Scotland and now became James I of England.

James wanted to unite his kingdom. But it was not until 1707 that the Act of Union joined England and Scotland together, with one **parliament**.

STUART TIMELINE

1603	James VI of Scotland becomes James I of England
1605	Gunpowder Plot
1642–1651	**Civil War**
1649	Charles I executed
1660	Charles II **restored** to the throne
1665–1666	Great Plague
1666	Great Fire of London
1707	Act of Union between England and Scotland
1714	End of Stuart rule with death of Queen Anne

Stuart Britain was a time of war and upheaval. It was also a time of great achievements in science, music, **literature**, and **architecture**. **Trade** flourished with countries overseas.

Successful trade meant coffee was introduced to Britain and coffee houses like this one opened.

GUNPOWDER PLOT

In 1605, there was a plot to blow up the king and Parliament in London as part of the struggle between **Roman Catholics** and **Protestants**. The plotters wanted to start a rebellion against the king. The plot was discovered when one of the group, Guy Fawkes, was found in a cellar beneath Parliament. This is still remembered on 5 November each year.

Civil war

These people are acting out a civil war battle.

When James I died in 1625, his son became king. Charles I argued with **Parliament** about how much power he should have. He wanted to rule by himself. This argument eventually led to **civil war** in England.

The war was fought between **Roundheads**, supporters of Parliament, and **Cavaliers**, supporters of the king. There were many battles in the civil war. In many places, ordinary people's homes were destroyed, and their animals and crops left to die.

In 1645, Charles I was defeated and taken prisoner. He was blamed for the deaths in the civil war and was beheaded in 1649. England was now a **republic**, without a king. In 1653, Oliver Cromwell became Lord Protector of the new Commonwealth of England. He set out to defeat Scotland and Ireland. But after Cromwell died, the Commonwealth fell apart. Charles I's son, Charles II, was **restored** to the throne in 1660.

OLIVER CROMWELL

Oliver Cromwell was a member of Parliament and also a brave and skilful leader. His New Model Army defeated the forces of Charles I at the Battle of Naseby in 1645. Cromwell took power as Lord Protector, but he refused to become king. He died in 1658.

What would my childhood be like?

In Stuart times, most people in Britain still lived in the countryside. If your family was poor, you had a hard time growing enough food to feed yourselves. You did not go to school but were expected to help your parents from a young age.

In 1601, Elizabeth I had passed a Poor Law. Overseers of the Poor collected a **tax**, called the Poor Rate. This money was used to help poor people in the **parish**. But poor people without jobs had to take whatever work they were given. If not, the "idle poor" (lazy poor) were often punished by whipping. Children whose parents had died were taken in by the parish, sent off to be **apprentices**, or sent to live with other families.

This painting shows children from a wealthy Royalist family (supporters of the king) being questioned by Cromwell's supporters.

Strict schooling

If you came from a wealthy family, you were sent to a petty (infant) school. At seven years old, many boys moved on to grammar schools. You had to work hard. If you made a mistake, you might be beaten with a birch made out of sharp twigs. Many girls learnt at home with their mothers.

These girls are having a music lesson. One girl is playing the violin and the other is playing the harpsichord.

BOARDING SCHOOLS

Some wealthy girls went to boarding schools in towns. They learnt reading, writing, music, dancing, sewing, and French.

Where would I live?

If your parents were very rich, you lived in a grand house. In Stuart times, people became interested in new styles of **architecture** and decoration from Italy, France, and Holland. Large houses had lots of glass windows and chimneys to show off their owners' wealth.

For children from poorer families, houses were small, with very basic furniture. Whole families often lived in houses with just one or two rooms. Some rich people built homes for the poor, or for old people. These were called almshouses.

These almshouses are in Alton, Hampshire.

This grand Stuart mansion in Birmingham was built between 1618 and 1635.

Stuart London

In Stuart times, London was the largest city in Britain. Many people moved to London from the countryside. Others came from abroad to work. London was dirty and overcrowded, although things did get better. From 1609, a network of pipes brought clean water into the city. But only wealthy people could afford to connect up their homes. Even then, the water was not clean enough to drink!

INIGO JONES

Inigo Jones was an important architect in Stuart times. In Italy, he studied ancient Roman ruins, and buildings by the Italian architect Andrea Palladio. He brought these ideas back to Britain.

What would I eat and drink?

Ordinary people ate a simple diet that had changed very little since medieval times. They lived on bread, porridge, and a kind of vegetable stew called **pottage**. They could not afford meat very often. In the countryside, people caught rabbits to cook for food.

This poor family is about to eat a meal.

Wealthier people ate richer food, with plenty of meat. In his diary for 1663, Samuel Pepys describes plates of rabbit, chicken, mutton (sheep), lamb, fish, pigeon, lobster, and various types of pie, all served at one meal! The main drink for poor people was a type of weak beer, while richer people drank wine.

Foreign food

New foods came from abroad to Stuart Britain. If your family could afford it, you could now eat bananas and pineapples. It also became fashionable to eat salads of raw, uncooked vegetables.

COFFEE HOUSES

People enjoyed new drinks in Stuart Britain – tea from China, cocoa (chocolate) from Mexico, and coffee from Arabia. Coffee was so popular that thousands of coffee houses grew up. These were places for people to meet, talk, do business, and read the newspapers.

What would I believe?

When James I came to the throne, England had broken away from the Catholic Church and was a **Protestant** country. But there were many groups with different religious beliefs. Some **Roman Catholics** hoped the new king would make Catholicism the official religion.

WITCHES

People sometimes blamed witchcraft for illnesses, bad luck, and other things that they did not really understand. A woman accused of being a witch was often tried in water. She was tied up and thrown in. If she sank, she was innocent. If she floated, she was guilty.

The Puritans

Other groups, such as the **Puritans**, thought that the Church of England was still too like the Roman Catholic Church. There were many Puritans in **Parliament** in the reign of Charles I, including Oliver Cromwell. During the Commonwealth, the Puritans closed down the theatres and made Sunday a strict day of worship.

Some Puritans left Britain to settle in places where they could worship freely. In 1620, over 100 people sailed from Plymouth in England on the *Mayflower*. They set up a Puritan settlement in America. Many other settlers followed after them.

Today, those who sailed on the *Mayflower* are known as the Pilgrim Fathers.

What clothes would I wear?

Early in the Stuart period, women wore wide, stiff skirts. They were held up by hoops of whalebone called farthingales. Around her neck, a fashionable lady had a stiff lace collar called a ruff. But after around 1620, clothes became more comfortable. The awkward farthingales disappeared. Skirts were long and flowing. Ruffs were replaced with wide, flat collars.

These wealthy Stuarts are wearing colourful Cavalier clothes.

Men wore **linen** shirts and fitted jackets called doublets. They wore short trousers, called breeches, stockings, and soft leather boots. Men had beards and grew their hair long. It was fashionable to have a strand of hair over one shoulder. This was called a lovelock. Later in the Stuart period, men shaved their faces and wore elaborate wigs on top of their own hair.

Both boys and girls wore long skirts until they were about five or six years old. Then boys started to wear breeches.

PLAIN AND SIMPLE

During the **civil war**, **Cavaliers** (supporters of the king) wore fashionable, colourful clothes. Supporters of **Parliament**, including many **Puritans**, wore much simpler, plainer clothes in dark colours.

This Puritan couple are wearing typically modest clothes.

What would happen if I was ill?

If you fell ill, you were probably looked after at home. Only wealthy people could afford to see a doctor. Even then, treatment was very basic. The most common cure was bloodletting. The doctor made a cut in your arm or leg and let your blood flow out into a bowl. This was meant to rid the body of poisons.

In Stuart times, thousands of people died of diseases, such as smallpox and the plague. People did not understand how disease spread. Many believed that sweet smells would drive disease away. During episodes of the plague, people carried flowers to try to avoid **infection**.

A plague doctor's mask was filled with herbs believed to protect him from disease.

Here, a victim of the Great Plague of London is lying in the street.

BATTLEFIELD SURGERY

Many people were injured and killed fighting in the **civil war**. Surgeons worked on the battlefields and tried to save the lives of injured soldiers. But many soldiers died from bleeding and infection.

The Great Plague

The Great Plague was a terrible disease that hit London in 1665. It killed over 100,000 people. Rats carried the fleas that caused the plague. But no one knew this then. Many people left London to try to escape the disease. The plague also struck in many other parts of the country.

What would I do when I grew up?

Poor children in the countryside and towns were expected to work from a young age. In the countryside, you helped your parents in the fields. Some children worked as servants. Others helped with jobs like ribbon-making, or worked as chimney sweeps.

Some children learnt a trade or a craft by becoming **apprentices**. You were not paid for your work, but you lived with your master (teacher) as part of the family. Poor children might be apprentices to butchers, blacksmiths, or millers. Children from richer families became apprentices in trades, such as printing, or to wealthy **merchants**.

Here a glass-maker and his apprentice are making windows.

As cities grew in Stuart times, more people needed houses, and fuel for heating. Industries such as brick-making, glass-making, and coal mining began to develop and become more important.

This wig-maker is combing one of his wigs.

NIT PICKERS

In his diary, Samuel Pepys describes being offered a wig full of nits (head lice). He refused it. One of the worst jobs in Stuart times was nit picker. Wealthy people paid nit pickers to remove the head lice from their wigs to make them clean!

How would I have fun?

In Stuart times, people liked to play cards and board games, such as chess and draughts. Children played with simple toys, including balls, spinning tops, and dolls.

Wealthy families played tennis and shuttlecock. They also liked to play palle-maille. This was a game played with a mallet and a ball. Players hit the ball through a hoop, rather like croquet. Charles II also had a royal yacht, which he liked to use for racing.

These boys are playing lots of different games, including bowling, palle-maille, and stilt walking.

Theatres

Many theatres opened in London during the reign of Elizabeth I. The theatres were closed down by Oliver Cromwell during the Commonwealth. But King Charles II loved the theatre. In 1662, he gave royal permission to two theatre companies to perform in London. They built theatres in Drury Lane and Covent Garden.

Newspapers also became popular in Stuart times. The *Daily Courant* was the first daily newspaper in Britain. It started in 1702.

PUNCH AND JUDY

In May 1662, Samuel Pepys wrote in his diary that he saw "an Italian puppet play". This is the first record of a Punch and Judy show. These shows were very popular in Stuart times.

After the Stuarts

Queen Anne reigned from 1702 to 1714. Anne was the last Stuart monarch because she died without any surviving children. The new king was George I, from the German family of Hanover. This marked the beginning of the Georgian period.

By the end of Anne's rule, Britain was a much wealthier place than at the start of Stuart times. In the late 1700s, farmers began to find better ways of growing crops. This meant they could grow more food. The Stuart period was also when Britain started to have **colonies** overseas. Many **merchants** became rich by **trading** with these colonies.

After the Act of Union, Queen Anne became the first ruler of Great Britain.

This is a painting of George I and his grandson, Prince Frederick.

ACT OF UNION

The Act of Union was passed by the **parliaments** of England and Scotland in 1707. It joined England, Wales, and Scotland together into the single state of Great Britain. This new state had one parliament, which met at Westminster in London. There were many reasons for the Act of Union, including as a way to secure peace. England was preparing to invade Scotland in 1706 if the Act was not passed.

How do we know?

In 1666, a year after the Great Plague, London was hit by another disaster. On 2 September, fire broke out at a baker's shop in Pudding Lane. At that time, most of the houses in London were made from wood. A strong wind quickly pushed the fire from house to house. Soon the sky was red with flames. It took four days to get the fire under control. Thousands of houses and buildings were burned down, and the city had to be rebuilt.

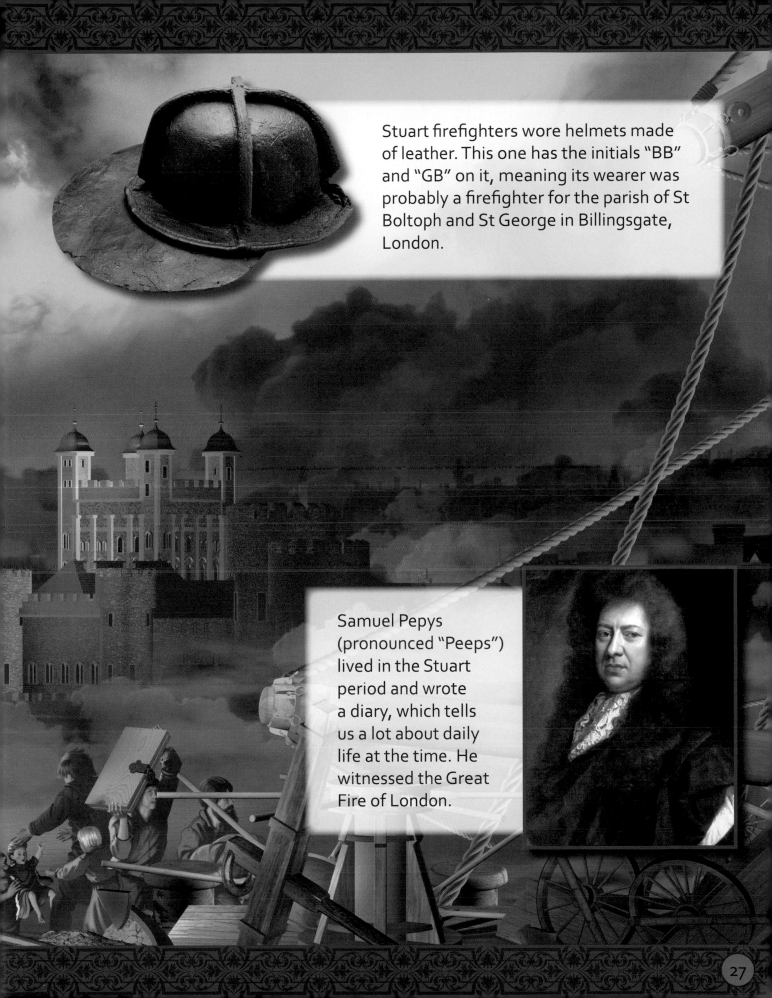

Stuart firefighters wore helmets made of leather. This one has the initials "BB" and "GB" on it, meaning its wearer was probably a firefighter for the parish of St Boltoph and St George in Billingsgate, London.

Samuel Pepys (pronounced "Peeps") lived in the Stuart period and wrote a diary, which tells us a lot about daily life at the time. He witnessed the Great Fire of London.

Family tree

FAMILY TREES EXPLAINED!

Lines going down mean the person below was the child of the person above. So James II was the son of Charles I.

The green line going sideways means the people married. So William III of Orange married Mary.

Stuart kings and queens

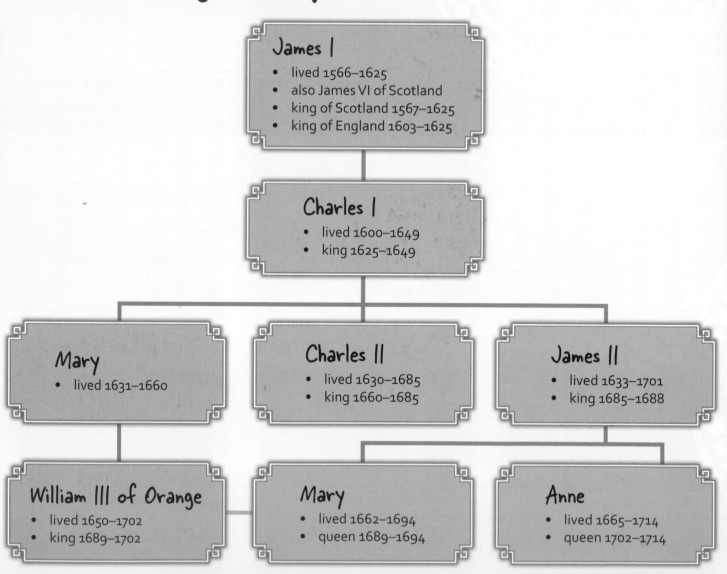

James I
- lived 1566–1625
- also James VI of Scotland
- king of Scotland 1567–1625
- king of England 1603–1625

Charles I
- lived 1600–1649
- king 1625–1649

Mary
- lived 1631–1660

Charles II
- lived 1630–1685
- king 1660–1685

James II
- lived 1633–1701
- king 1685–1688

William III of Orange
- lived 1650–1702
- king 1689–1702

Mary
- lived 1662–1694
- queen 1689–1694

Anne
- lived 1665–1714
- queen 1702–1714

Quiz

What do you know about life in Stuart times? Try this quiz to find out!

1. What was the Act of Union of 1707?
    a an agreement to join England and Scotland
    b a royal marriage
    c an agreement to join England and Wales

2. What happened to Charles I?
    a he lived happily to a ripe old age
    b he went mad
    c he had his head cut off

3. Where did merchants go to do business in Stuart London?
    a the office
    b the coffee house
    c the hairdressers

4. In Stuart times, what was a lovelock?
    a a fashionable hairstyle for men
    b a type of hug
    c a type of key

5. How did the Great Plague spread?
    a by bad smells
    b by cats and dogs
    c by fleas on rats

Answers
1. a
2. c
3. b
4. a
5. c

Glossary

apprentice person who is learning a trade

architecture design of a building

Cavalier supporter of the king in the English Civil War

civil war war between people of the same country

colony country governed by another country, often quite far away

infection spreading disease from one person to another

linen cloth made from the flax plant

literature books and other writing

merchant person who buys and sells goods

parish church district with its own church building and priest

parliament group of people who are elected by a country to make laws

pottage type of thick soup made from oats and vegetables

Protestant Christian who began to question the teachings of the Roman Catholic Church in the 1500s and demanded changes

Puritan English Protestant who thought that the reforms of the Church of England had not gone far enough

republic government where the head of state is not a king or queen

restore bring back. In 1660, the Stuarts were restored to the throne when Charles I's son was asked to rule the country as King Charles II.

Roman Catholic Church based in Rome, which has the Pope as its head

Roundhead supporter of Parliament in the English Civil War

tax money taken by government from people's earnings, or from money earned by selling things

trade buying and selling goods

Tudor royal family that ruled Britain from 1485 until 1603

Find out more

Books

Horribly Famous: Oliver Cromwell and his Not-So Civil War, Alan MacDonald (Scholastic, 2010)

The Story of the Great Fire of London, Anita Ganeri (Raintree, 2008)

Tudors and Stuarts (Usborne History of Britain), Fiona Patchett (Usborne, 2008)

Websites

www.schoolsliaison.org.uk/kids/aston/stuarts/stuarts.htm
The Birmingham Museums and Art Gallery website has information about the Stuarts and the civil war in England.

www.royal.gov.uk/HistoryoftheMonarchy/ KingsandQueensoftheUnitedKingdom/TheStuarts/TheStuarts.aspx
The official website of the British monarchy has facts and figures about the Stuart kings and queens.

www.museumoflondon.org.uk/Explore-online/Past/LondonsBurning
The Museum of London's website is packed with pictures, information, and eyewitness accounts of the Great Fire of London.

Places to visit

There are many Stuart houses to visit all over Britain. You can find out about them through the following organizations:

English Heritage
www.english-heritage.org.uk

The National Trust in England, Wales, and Northern Ireland
www.nationaltrust.org.uk

The National Trust of Scotland
www.nts.org.uk

Index